the lion is safe. "'Safe?' said Mr. Beaver. 'Don't you hear what Mrs. Beaver tells you? Who said anything about safe? 'Course he isn't safe. But he's good. He's the King, I tell you.'"

Following Jesus is anything but safe. Then again, do we really want to get to the end of our lives and say, "Wow, I sure played it really safe"?

Look for your Open Door. It may not be safe, but when God is in it, it is good.

"He's the King, I tell you."

"AGAIN JESUS SAID, 'PEACE BE WITH YOU! AS THE FATHER HAS SENT ME, I AM SENDING YOU.'"

—John 20:21

Very rarely in the Bible does God come to someone and say, "Stay." Almost never does God interrupt someone and ask them to remain in comfort, safety, and familiarity. He opens a door and calls them to come through it.

ALL THE PLACES TO GO . . .

HOW WILL YOU KNOW?

P. 13

DAY 1

Open Doors

MOVE!

In physics we know an object at rest tends to stay at rest, and an object in motion tends to stay in motion. Our tendency to remain inactive is the result of inertia. It is hard to move if we are sitting still. Like a rocket at liftoff, the greatest need for energy is to get off the ground. The engines roar, and the surge is slow at first, but the rocket inches higher and faster toward a heavenly destination.

The toughest step to commit to exercise is the one needed to walk out the door. Once we're moving, energy begins to surge. Movement is so much easier once we are already moving.

The toughest part of Open Doors is today. Today is the first day; today is takeoff. Today is overcoming your stillness. Today is like trying to steer a parked car. Cars are really hard to steer while sitting still; they only turn when you are moving. The steering wheel of your life won't move if you're not also moving. Today is about overcoming inertia.

God has demonstrated that he is willing to move to us. The Father sent Jesus to us. Jesus was willing to move from his rightful place with the Father to demonstrate his love for us. As the Father sent Jesus, he now sends us to demonstrate his love to others.

I've heard it said that inspiration shows up when we do. We get comfortable. We hold on to the familiar. We wait for God to inspire us to move. Yet, if you move toward that Open Door, even when you don't feel up to it at the moment, inspiration hits. God will give grace and energy to your movement. God will multiply your spiritual energy. God, as well as your inspiration, will show up.

Prayer: *Lord, help me to live for more than comfort and familiarity. Give me energy to walk through a new door that you have opened. Save me from being stagnant, and help my movement to bring new filters into my life. Help me to learn, love, and experience you as I move toward a new place.*

“MY **STEPS** HAVE HELD TO YOUR PATHS; MY FEET HAVE NOT STUMBLED.”

—Psalm 17:5

There’s an old saying for travelers. A car’s headlights only shine for fifteen feet, but that fifteen feet will get you all the way home. God knows just how much clarity will be good for us—not too much, and not too little. We don’t follow clarity. We follow God.

ALL THE PLACES TO GO . . .

HOW WILL YOU KNOW?

P. 245

DAY 2

Open Doors

THE NEXT STEP

If you're reading this, congratulations! You have overcome inertia, and you are moving forward. Now, day 2: the next step.

The next step involves putting one foot in front of the other and moving forward. There are times when we feel paralyzed because we cannot see the steps we need to take in the future: fifty, one hundred, or even one thousand steps from now. Not being able to see the path around the bend may make us uneasy or unsure about the journey. Because we can't see future steps, we are slow to take the next step.

We often ask God to give us an unrestricted view beyond the open door. There are times, however, when he simply shows us the next step and not the complete map. He knows we can stumble when we're looking too far down the path.

When my middle son was a young boy, we were walking along a path to get to the state fair. Coming upon a substantial puddle with standing water, he hesitated to take the next step to cross the hazard. There was no way to go around. He had to go over it. My wife, seeing his confusion, knew he needed help getting across. She didn't simply give instruction but told Noah to watch where she stepped as she went ahead of him and he could get to the other side. As she walked in front of him she said, "Step here . . . then here . . . then here, and you'll get across." He wasn't simply told how to walk but was given the places to cross over.

God gives us the light to see the next step. Step after step, we make progress on the journey. Open-door living requires taking the next step. Jesus is walking in front of you to show you the way.

Prayer: *Lord, today show me the next step toward my Open Door. Give me a heart that is willing to take the next step without completely knowing every future step. Keep my destination in front of me, but give me strength today to take the next step.*

> NOW FAITH IS CONFIDENCE IN WHAT WE HOPE FOR AND ASSURANCE ABOUT WHAT WE DO NOT SEE.
>
> —*Hebrews 11:1*

Jesus comes to people and invites us to be what-if? *people. He said to his early followers, "I want you to imagine a kingdom—the* real *magic kingdom. Imagine a kingdom where the last are first, the least are greatest, the servants are heroes, the weak are strong, and the marginalized are loved and cherished.*

Imagine a world where outsiders become insiders, where people who lose their lives end up finding them, where people who die to themselves and their guilt and their sin and their selfishness end up being brought to life. Imagine that your little broken story can become part of a larger story that ends well."

ALL THE PLACES TO GO . . .

HOW WILL YOU KNOW?

P. 61

DAY 3

Open Doors

WHAT IF?

In grammar, there is a technique in which the normal order of words is reversed to give emphasis or to maintain meter or rhyme. It's called inversion. Dr. Seuss wrote in this way to help us see life differently. The seemingly nonsensical words, worlds, and rhymes he created were, as he put it, "a way of looking at life through the wrong end of a telescope."

Jesus was constantly giving us a principle of inversion for life. He changes the order. Inversion means that the apparent way of living is not the real way to live. The first become last. What looks like much is actually little, and what seems to be little can be much.

So what if we embrace the inversion that God has for us? What if we see things as God sees them? What if we are servants so we can become leaders, and we embrace our weakness so we can be strong?

God flips the script in the most amazing ways. The light of God's love shined brightest on the day that was midnight dark. Joy unspeakable was found when agony beyond description was on full display. The Father hid his face from the Son so that we, aliens and strangers, could become children of God.

For Open-Door people, "what-if" is not simply conjecture. It is how we flip the telescope and live inverted lives. What if God would do the unthinkable? God took on earthly form, then stormed hell that we might be elevated to heavenly places. Now it's not "What if?" but "It is done!"

Prayer: *Lord, help us to see the inverted reality of the gospel. May we know your strength as we acknowledge our weakness. Show us open doors that seem opposite of the world's view but are actually portals to experience your grace.*

> “ABRAM BELIEVED THE LORD, AND HE CREDITED IT TO HIM AS RIGHTEOUSNESS.”

—*Genesis 15:6*

Just about every parent I've ever known, when they get that first kid home, finds him- or herself thinking, I don't think I'm ready for this. *Then that kid grows up, and it's time for the kid to leave home and face the world, but the world is scary and expensive, and the kid says, "I don't think I'm ready for this." And the parents say, "Ready or not . . ."*

There's a whole syndrome around this fear called "failure to launch." People are often afraid to go through economic independence, vocational direction, and relational open doors because they don't feel ready. But the world says, "Ready or not, here I come."

ALL THE PLACES TO GO . . .

HOW WILL YOU KNOW?

P. 26

DAY 4

Open Doors

ARE YOU READY?

You've heard it said, "There is never a good time to . . ." You can finish that sentence a number of ways: there is never a good time to say good-bye; there is never a good time to breakup.

In his book *He's Just Not That into You*, Greg Berhendt gives insight into being ready to get married. He says, "There will never be a good time, financially, to get married, unless you're Shaq or Ray Romano. But somehow people manage."

For most life-altering moments, it never really feels like we're ready. When do you really know you're ready to get married, have a baby, change jobs, start a company, or begin a ministry? We always have reasons to wait, and many are even legitimate.

There is never a good time to walk through an open door.

When God called Abram to leave Ur and possess the land, he was already 75 years old! Not only this, but he was told his descendants would be "more than the stars in the sky"—even though he was an old man married to an old woman, and they had no children. His circumstances, to say the least, did not give him much confidence.

But Abram said, "Sovereign Lord, how can I know that I will gain possession of it?" (Genesis 15:8).

God answered like our parents do: "because I said so." He promised Abram the land and many descendants. He sealed his promise by entering into a covenant with Abram. Abram's confidence would not be based completely on understanding his circumstances but on God's promises.

As long as readiness is defined by a perfect set of circumstances or completely understanding why, we will never be ready. We never launch. Readiness is a focus of faith. Readiness isn't having every detail in place before we launch. It may sound cliché, but we are ready because God promises to be there. We have faith in a perfect God, not perfect circumstances.

Prayer: *Lord, may our readiness be focused on you rather than our circumstances. Let us be ready to trust you. When we can't see beyond the Open Door, let us trust your promise to be faithful. May we trust that your love for us is stronger than any other circumstance in our lives.*

“TRULY I TELL YOU, IF YOU HAVE FAITH AS SMALL AS A MUSTARD SEED, YOU CAN SAY TO THIS MOUNTAIN, ‘MOVE FROM HERE TO THERE,’ AND IT WILL MOVE. NOTHING WILL BE IMPOSSIBLE FOR YOU.”

—*Matthew 17:20*

DAY 5

Open Doors

SMALL STUFF

The Kingdom of God is made up of lots and lots of small stuff. We do big things for God when we understand how to do lots of little things. Faith the size of a mustard seed produces mountain-moving faith. The widow giving her two small coins was the greatest example of generosity according to Jesus: small gift, big sacrifice. If you are to be faithful in much, you must first be faithful in little.

> Think of something big. A mountain? A tree? . . . Now, consider that it is made up of tiny, tiny atoms. Atoms are made up of even tinier neutrons and protons. Neutrons and protons are made up of elements so small that they can't be seen with the strongest microscope. No such thing as big. Everything we call "big" is just a whole lot of "small." There is no big without lots and lots of small. Nature as God created it is the image of the invisible Kingdom of Heaven. In Kingdom living, small matters. Small is the key to big.[1]

God often infuses small things with big power. A simple shepherd's staff transformed Moses into the liberator of the children of Israel. David dropped a large giant with five smooth stones. A small child brought fish and loaves so Jesus could multiply the small offering and feed thousands.

We can dismiss our small as insignificant. Better yet, having our small available to God can make it an agent of transformation. Little faith in a big God moves mountains. An insignificant shepherd's staff can part the sea. A little boy's lunch can feed a hungry crowd. As the song says, "little is much when God is in it."

What's that in your hand? Give God your small and watch him do something big.

Prayer: *Lord, help us to give you everything in our lives, in particular our small stuff. If our talent is small, it is yours to multiply. Take our insignificant and make it substantial. Today, may we be faithful with our small steps leading to open doors.*

1 Jennifer Kennedy Dean, "Think Small When You Dream Big," Praying Life Foundation, April 13, 2011, http://prayinglife.org/2011/04/think-small-when-you-drean-big

"SEARCH ME, GOD,
AND KNOW MY HEART;
TEST ME AND
KNOW MY ANXIOUS
THOUGHTS.

SEE IF THERE IS ANY
OFFENSIVE WAY IN ME,
AND LEAD ME IN THE
WAY EVERLASTING."

—Psalm 139:23-24

"I GAIN
UNDERSTANDING
FROM YOUR PRECEPTS;
THEREFORE I HATE
EVERY WRONG PATH.

YOUR WORD IS A LAMP
FOR MY FEET, A LIGHT
ON MY PATH."

—Psalm 119:104-105

DAY 6

Open Doors

RUNNING THE WRONG WAY

Jim Marshall is a Hall of Fame lineman who played for the Minnesota Vikings. He played twenty years in the NFL as one of the "Purple People Eaters." He was one of the finest linemen of the sixties and seventies. Except on one play.

On October 25, 1964, as the Vikings were playing the San Francisco 49ers, Marshall picked up a fumble and realized he had a clear shot to the end zone. One problem: it was the wrong end zone. Instead of scoring a touchdown for his team, he scored a safety for the 49ers.

"My first inkling that something was wrong was when a 49ers player gave me a hug in the end zone," stated Marshall.

There are so many problems when we run the wrong way: we score for the wrong team; we are dazed and confused. Running the wrong way in a football game is a problem. Going east on a westbound interstate can be catastrophic.

Like football and cars, we can run the wrong way in life. At times, we don't even know we are heading in the wrong direction. There is an Afghan proverb that says, "If you think you're leading and no one is following you, then you're only taking a walk." If you're running and no one is chasing you, you're probably running the wrong way.

The only thing worse than running the wrong way is doing nothing. Perhaps as a result of running the wrong way in our past, we sit on the sidelines, afraid to get in the game. "Princeton philosopher Walter Kaufmann coined the word *decidophobia*. He noticed that human beings are afraid of making decisions. We don't want the anxiety that goes along with the possibility of being wrong. Decisions wear us out" (*All the Places to Go . . . How Will You Know?*, p. 107).

We all have the capacity to run the wrong way. We need a lamp for our feet and a light for our paths. Life can leave our heads spinning, and we can lose our bearings. God alone can give us a spiritual GPS to send us in the right direction. In fact, if not for God's grace, we would all run the wrong way. Do you need to turn around today? Does someone you love need to make a U-turn? We all have gone our own ways, but God gives us the way everlasting.

Prayer: *Lord, give me direction. Give me discernment. Give me courage. Lead me in the way everlasting and not in the way that leads to destruction. Save me from the fear of mistakes that leads to spiritual lethargy. Let me run and not grow weary.*

“JESUS WENT OUT AND SAW A TAX COLLECTOR BY THE NAME OF LEVI SITTING AT HIS TAX BOOTH. ‘FOLLOW ME,’ JESUS SAID TO HIM, AND LEVI GOT UP, LEFT EVERYTHING AND FOLLOWED HIM.”

—Luke 5:27-28

“TO GRASP HOW WIDE AND LONG AND HIGH AND DEEP IS THE LOVE OF CHRIST, AND TO KNOW THIS LOVE THAT SURPASSES KNOWLEDGE—THAT YOU MAY BE FILLED TO THE MEASURE OF ALL THE FULLNESS OF GOD.”

—Ephesians 3:18-19

DAY 7

Open Doors

DIMENSION

As a child, the simple pleasure of lying on our backs, gazing heavenward and marveling at the stars is one reason they were called 'the wonder years.' Even now, decades removed from those wonder years, I'm captured by the vastness and greatness that glittering nights still reveal about God. There is majesty to the revelation.

There is a power that produces awe.

There is also something missing.

We can get lost in the vastness of the majestic revelation. We lack dimension and have a hard time relating. Yes, there is something missing. It speaks volumes about God, but at times, it's too loud. Where is the still, small voice?

Creation shouts truth about God. It's loud and apparent but has gaps in communication. At times in life, shouting can be disorienting. Shouting happens when someone is far away. Shouting is needed when other noises clutter the airwaves. Shouting happens when nuance goes straight over my head. Shouting assumes I have a hard time understanding or hearing, or I didn't get it the first time.

There is an otherness to creation. That otherness points to an awesome power, but it also points to how different that power is from you and me. With God's otherness, there is an inherent distance. If that's all we have, we don't always have context to understand God. His ways are not our ways. When we see creation, the otherness of God is apparent. It is amazing, but it creates a yearning more than satisfying the heart.

Creation points to power, and often you and I feel impotent. Creation points to greatness, and often we feel insignificant. Creation reveals majesty when you and I feel like anything but majestic. The fumbling, stumbling, bumbling existence that life can be doesn't relate to the ease when God said "light," and then there was light in the darkness. My words don't have that power.

Then Jesus came and said, "Follow me." The abstract became tangible; that which is beyond knowledge became knowable. The infinite gave me something finite to chew on. The transcendent took on dimension. The dimension God gave us didn't limit as much as it gave us intimacy. Something—better yet, someone—we can get our arms around.

Prayer: *God, you are awesome, and you are worthy of our awe. Thank you for Jesus, who has given us a perfect dimension to an infinite God. Thank you that Jesus demonstrates a love beyond comprehension and grace beyond compare. May we walk through open doors because Jesus takes our hands and leads us. In Jesus, we have dimension to grasp how wide, how long, how high, how deep your love is.*

"IF ANY OF YOU LACKS WISDOM, YOU SHOULD ASK GOD, WHO GIVES GENEROUSLY TO ALL WITHOUT FINDING FAULT, AND IT WILL BE GIVEN TO YOU."

—*James 1:5*

"DOES NOT WISDOM CALL OUT?
DOES NOT UNDERSTANDING RAISE HER VOICE?

AT THE HIGHEST POINT ALONG THE WAY,
WHERE THE PATHS MEET, SHE TAKES HER STAND;

BESIDE THE GATE LEADING INTO THE CITY,
AT THE ENTRANCE, SHE CRIES ALOUD:

"TO YOU, O PEOPLE, I CALL OUT;
I RAISE MY VOICE TO ALL MANKIND.

YOU WHO ARE SIMPLE, GAIN PRUDENCE;
YOU WHO ARE FOOLISH, SET YOUR HEARTS ON IT.

LISTEN, FOR I HAVE TRUSTWORTHY THINGS TO SAY;
OPEN MY LIPS TO SPEAK WHAT IS RIGHT."

—*Proverbs 8:1-6*

DAY 8

Open Doors
WISDOM

Anyone who has seen the television show *Let's Make a Deal* realizes the importance of doors in the show. The final climatic deal for the show ends with two contestants choosing between three doors for the top prize.

High drama ensues as the contestants struggle to choose the right door. At times, the contestants will gamble and choose the unknown behind the door, so afraid to miss the opportunity for something really big. *Sure, I've got cash in my hand, but consider the possibilities.* For others, a "bird in the hand" is better. *Why lose a perfectly good washer dryer for the chance to win the dream vacation of a lifetime?* It's fascinating how we struggle with decisions and doors.

By now, the studio audience members are screaming suggestions at the top of their lungs. They're well-intentioned people who are trying to help, but they're simply adding to the chaos. From the audience's perspective, of course the contestants should go for it. After all, what do they have to lose? Interesting how someone who doesn't have to live with the consequences of a decision can make our choices seem so simple.

With all the shouting, which voice do we hear when we stand before that door? Have you ever stood before a door, confused and afraid to act? Maybe well-intentioned friends have given you advice, but it only adds to the confusion. The voice we must hear is God's wisdom.

When you stand before more than one door, the request should be for wisdom. More than revealing a simple formula, God tells you and me to ask for wisdom. Wisdom stakes out high ground and narrows our path. We can hear God speak in Scripture, as his Spirit convicts and convinces. He assures and warns. He guides and encourages. Amid all the voices, wisdom speaks and is not silent. If we lack wisdom, God says we simply need to ask, and he will give it generously. Wow—such a deal!

Prayer: *Lord, teach us to know your voice when we stand before more than one door. Please stand where the paths come together. Quiet the noise. Give us ears to hear. Be generous with your wisdom. Feed us with your Word.*

> **"** DAVID SAID TO SAUL, 'LET NO ONE LOSE HEART ON ACCOUNT OF THIS PHILISTINE; YOUR SERVANT WILL GO AND FIGHT HIM.' **"**
>
> —*1 Samuel 17:32*

Often an open door to another room begins with a sense of discontent about the room you're already in.

—

"I know that your strength is small," God says to the church at Philadelphia. People in the church may not have been hugely flattered when they read that line. But what a gift to know that open doors are not reserved for the especially talented or the extraordinarily strong. God can open a door for anyone.

ALL THE PLACES TO GO . . .

HOW WILL YOU KNOW?

P. 5, 7

DAY 9

Open Doors
DISCONTENTMENT

The giant taunts God's people. No one will step up to the challenge, until the shepherd boy can take it no more. At what point do you and I say "no more"? The taunts of the giant must be silenced.

Does your soul ache for a cause? You and I don't have to be especially talented or extraordinarily strong to address the problem. God calls your ordinary self to make a difference. To be discontent is to realize that we live in a broken world. We could hope our brokenness will be made whole by politicians or big-name preachers or even superheroes, but we know better.

Mike Daniels of Atlas Ministry was a veterinarian, yet a holy discontent burned in his heart to help families and children who were trapped in the cycle of poverty. Mike believes we must make solutions local and not wait on the next political election to give us answers. He created an organization that mentors parents and partners with public schools to address teen pregnancy, literacy, and graduation rates. Mike didn't complain about the culture but let his discontentment move him to be a change agent. He couldn't stand being in the room of complacency any longer, simply sitting in the darkness.

His open door was a simmering discontent. He didn't call others and point to the open door so they would make a difference. His discontent was his alone, and so was his open door.

Next time you're tempted to say, "What is our world coming to?" simply stop. The burning discontent is evidence that we are made for more than cursing the darkness. We are made to make a difference, to give light, and to show mercy. Find your five smooth stones, for you and I are made to knock down giants.

Prayer: *Lord, help me to burn with discontentment for the injustice in our world. Give me a heart to move quickly and not depend on others to solve problems. With open arms I bring all I have to make a difference. By your grace, may my discontent fuel action for those who need to experience the love of Jesus.*

"ASK AND IT WILL BE GIVEN TO YOU; SEEK AND YOU WILL FIND; KNOCK AND THE DOOR WILL BE OPENED TO YOU. FOR EVERYONE WHO ASKS RECEIVES; THE ONE WHO SEEKS FINDS; AND TO THE ONE WHO KNOCKS, THE DOOR WILL BE OPENED."

—*Matthew 7:7-8*

DAY 10

Open Doors

THRESHOLD

To walk through an open door means to cross a threshold. Literally, a threshold is the strip of wood, metal, or stone at the base of a door. *Threshold* also means the point at which change is produced. This is what we mean when we say someone has a low or high threshold for pain.

Thresholds are points of entry for change. A husband may carry a bride across the threshold to symbolize that two separate lives will now become one. It is a sign of trust and commitment to one another.

Do we have a high or low threshold for trust? Do we have a high or low threshold for forgiveness? Do we have a high or low threshold for peace? A high threshold for pain is good. Not so much when we are talking about the level of stimulus needed to trust, forgive, or be at peace.

Open-door living requires us to ask and keep on asking, to knock and keep on knocking, to seek and keep on seeking.

Perhaps this day, you stand at a new threshold. Maybe it is the threshold of a new relationship or a new job or a new ministry. Better yet, today may be a day to discover a threshold you cannot name at this moment. Walk through that threshold with gusto.

Today, believe in the same God who has brought you across the greatest threshold you'll ever experience: crossing the threshold from death into life. If he carried you out of the darkness into his marvelous light, you can cross any threshold you face today.

Prayer: *Lord, I am asking you to give me the faith and guidance I need to cross over the threshold into a life filled with trust, forgiveness, and peace. Move me out of my small rooms of doubt, fear, or comfort to cross over to a life where I am filled by your Spirit.*

One of the big problems with open doors is that they're not always well marked. When God does call, the call may not always be clear. As a general rule, with God, information is given on a need-to-know basis, and God decides who needs to know what, when.

ALL THE PLACES TO GO . . .

HOW WILL YOU KNOW?

P. 29

DAY 11

Open Doors

UNCERTAINTY

We always seem to have issues when we are certain about mysterious things and find mystery in things certain.

The Pharisees were really good at reducing the mystery of a great God to a certain moral code. On the other hand, our enlightened culture is constantly trying to create uncertainty around the gospel. The skeptical culture questions, "Jesus wasn't really uniquely God in the flesh, right? Perhaps he didn't physically rise from the grave—it was only a spiritual resurrection, right?"

We get in trouble when we mix up the mysterious with the certain and vice versa.

The certainty of the gospel is something on which we can build our trust in eternity. Paul tells us that if Jesus wasn't raised from the dead, we live under a cruel delusion. He wants you to know the certainty of Jesus as God in the flesh and as God over death.

We also tend to make the mysterious things of God in our everyday lives way too certain. Trying to interpret our circumstances with certainty can make the Christian life formulaic. Say the right words or perform the right ritual, and God is absolutely bound to do the fixed outcome.

Really?

If we are to walk by faith, our daily decisions will be made with some level of mystery. Open-door people have to get comfortable with mystery. At times, we must be willing to live with some level of ambiguity.

> *"From the beginning of God's interactions with humanity, he seems to give information on a need-to-know basis. Ambiguity and uncertainty are woven into the story from the beginning. The first eleven chapters of Genesis involve big themes: Creation, Fall, Judgment—but all that is leading to a moment in Genesis 12 when things narrow down to the smallest scale. God is going to come now to one ordinary individual. Not a king on a giant stage—just one regular person. It could be you. It could be me. We never know ahead of time the full significance of the doors we face."*
>
> *—All the Places to Go . . . How Will You Know?*, p. 30

Prayer: *Father, give us faith to embrace the certainty of the gospel. Heaven and earth will pass away, but your Word will remain forever. With the foundation of that certainty, give us faith to embrace the mystery of life. Help us to be comfortable in the ambiguity that often is necessary to experience you.*

"CONSIDER IT PURE JOY, MY BROTHERS AND SISTERS, WHENEVER YOU FACE TRIALS OF MANY KINDS, BECAUSE YOU KNOW THAT THE TESTING OF YOUR FAITH PRODUCES PERSEVERANCE. LET PERSEVERANCE FINISH ITS WORK SO THAT YOU MAY BE MATURE AND COMPLETE, NOT LACKING ANYTHING. IF ANY OF YOU LACKS WISDOM, YOU SHOULD ASK GOD, WHO GIVES GENEROUSLY TO ALL WITHOUT FINDING FAULT, AND IT WILL BE GIVEN TO YOU."

—*James 1:2-5*

You need a God-sized problem. If you don't have one, your current problem is you don't have a problem. Life is facing and solving problems. When God calls people, he calls them to face a problem. The standard word for the condition of being truly problem-free is dead.

ALL THE PLACES TO GO . . .

HOW WILL YOU KNOW?

P. 118

Open Doors

WHAT'S YOUR PROBLEM?

"It's your world. The rest of us are just renting."

We might use that phrase if we make life all about ourselves. *Narcissistic* is probably too strong of a word (or is it?), but we certainly lose perspective when we define issues and problems by our personal worlds only.

What do your problems say about you? Are your problems simply about taking care of you and yours? Is it really just your world that concerns you? While addressing the priority of your world is necessary, shouldn't your problems be greater than yourself?

Listen to John in *All the Places to Go . . . How Will You Know?*:

> People with small souls have small problems: how to make their lives safer or more convenient; how to put an irritating neighbor in his or her place; how to make wrinkles less visible; how to cope with cranky coworkers or lack of recognition. Small people are occupied by small problems. People who live with largeness of soul are occupied by large problems. How to end extreme poverty; how to stop sex trafficking; how to help at-risk children receive a great education; how to bring beauty and art to a city. (p. 117–118)

Today, find a problem. Ask God to give you insight, wisdom, and courage to walk through an open door, and then watch God begin to solve the problem.

Prayer: *Lord, build my faith as you take down my problems. Don't let me settle for petty problems. Let me find ways to solve problems for my family, for my community, for my country, and even for the world. Give me courage to tackle bigger problems as you provide open doors for me to walk through.*

“FOR WE LIVE BY FAITH, NOT BY SIGHT.”

—2 Corinthians 5:7

In other words, often what matters most is not the decision I make but how I throw myself into executing it well. It's better to go through the wrong door with your best self than the best door with your wrong self. Sometimes the way in which I go through the door matters more than which door I actually go through.

ALL THE PLACES TO GO . . .

HOW WILL YOU KNOW?

P. 135

Open Doors

WRONG DOOR

Walking through the wrong door usually isn't pleasant. Finding open doors isn't an exact science. So, what do you do if you walk through the wrong door?

Wrong doors can encourage growth or can leave us struggling with regret. Choosing the wrong open door can be a dramatic learning event. If it produces paralyzing regret, however, we simply sit down in the wrong room, fixating on our bad choices.

Living in regret "is a form of what social scientists refer to as 'counterfactual thinking,' where people who don't like the outcome of one decision obsess over what might have happened in an alternative hypothetical scenario. The classic phrase is 'If only . . .' 'If only I'd taken that job/dated that person/chosen that school/made that investment instead of this one'" (*All the Places to Go . . . How Will You Know?*, p. 98).

When we walk through the wrong doors, pain will typically be the end result. Yet, while pain isn't an end in itself, it can be a catalyst for change. With wrong doors, it is normal say, "I don't want to do that again." Hopefully it would also be normal to say, "I don't want to be the same person I was before I walked through that door."

"God's primary will for your life is not the achievements you accrue; it's the person you become" (*All the Places to Go . . . How Will You Know?*, p. 15). Right door or wrong door, sometimes it is hard to know which one it is. Make sure it is a door you don't walk through alone. Make sure God changes you. Whether you spirit soars with gratitude for God's blessing or whether God's grace becomes more apparent as things start falling down around you, trust and cling to him.

Right door or wrong door? Make sure it is a "be more like Jesus" door.

Prayer: *Lord, help me to have grace to know the wrong doors in my life. Give me grace to move to a new room and not simply sit down in regret. In the right doors, give me gratitude. In the wrong doors, give me instruction; give me strength to face the challenge. Through any door, make me more like Jesus.*

> "BUT THANKS BE TO GOD, WHO ALWAYS LEADS US AS CAPTIVES IN CHRIST'S TRIUMPHAL PROCESSION AND USES US TO SPREAD THE AROMA OF THE KNOWLEDGE OF HIM EVERYWHERE."

—2 Corinthians 2:14

It is an open door, symbolic of "boundless opportunities. Of unlimited chances to do something worthwhile; of grand openings into new and unknown adventures of significant living; of heretofore unimagined chances to do good, to make our lives count for eternity." An open door is the great adventure of life because it means the possibility of being useful to God.

ALL THE PLACES TO GO . . .

HOW WILL YOU KNOW?

P. 5

Open Doors

BEING USEFUL TO GOD

"Being useful to God"—what an amazing proposition! This notion has so many possibilities. God, the source of all life, joy, and beauty, desires to use us in his own way. How can we be useful to God? We can extend grace in a moment of painful regret or beauty in places of pervasive ugliness. We can offer meaning in seemingly random moments. We can show love where hate rules.

We all have moments when we feel irrelevant. Maybe being the newbie in a strange setting or swimming upstream when the current of opinion is strong in the other direction. As people age, the hurt is apparent when they speak of being treated as irrelevant. When dismissed as not understanding the latest technology or knowing pop culture, we dismiss the deep wisdom the years have taught. It hurts if we don't feel useful.

How wonderful it is to be useful to God and not irrelevant!

The goal of *All the Places to Go . . . How Will You Know?* and the Open Doors Campaign is to create a context in which you can be "useful to God." This isn't about simply filling a role at the church. You probably know your gifts and your ministry passion. More useful than knowledge, however, is a call to action.

There is a deep satisfaction that comes from using the gifts God has designed for you. While you've heard those words before, today could be the day to take the first step to actually living out that reality. As friends say to one another when someone is just standing around while others are working, "Hey, make yourself useful."

God is working. Substantial, even eternal work. Today, make yourself useful.

Prayer: *Lord, make us useful to you this day. Help us to love when love is in great shortage. Help us to give grace when someone is drowning in regret. In a world filled with ugliness, may we bring your beauty. Lord, I am desperate to be useful to you. Save me from an irrelevant life. Please make this day, this week, this month useful to you.*

NOTES

NOTES

NOTES